Don't Count The Yes's, Count The No's

~ *and* ~

Time Management Skills That Work

Don't Count the Yes's, Count the No's

~and~

Time Management Skills That Work

By Warren Greshes

MEDIA

MEDIA

Published 2018 by Gildan Media LLC
aka G&D Media
www.GandDmedia.com

FIRST EDITION 2018

Front Cover design by David Rheinhardt of Pyrographx

Interior design by Meghan Day Healey of Story Horse, LLC

Library of Congress Cataloging-in-Publication Data is available upon request

ISBN: 978-1-7225-0021-4

10   9   8   7   6   5   4   3   2   1

Contents

Don't Count the Yes's, Count the No's

Contents

Introduction

Selling is rejection, plain and simple. The top sales people can deal with it; the rest can't.

Ask any sales VP or sales manager and they'll all tell you the same thing. The biggest reason their sales people do not bring in enough business is that they don't see enough people. They don't see enough people because they fear rejection. They fear rejection because they don't know how much rejection they need.

In this book, we're going to cover five important areas of prospecting:

1. why prospecting and generating consistent every day activity is so important
2. how to handle rejection by understanding how much rejection you need
3. how to prepare for and make the prospecting call
4. how to anticipate, handle, and turnaround objections
5. why you need to practice every day.

If you implement the ideas, and use the Action Guide, which you can find at the end of this book, here's what will happen. You will handle rejection better than you ever have, which will enable you to make more calls, speak to more decision makers, sell more appointments and make more presentations, and the greatest benefit of all, close more sales and make more money.

The purpose of this book is to help you sell appointments and get yourself in front of prospects. While that may seem simple, most sales people never truly comprehend or they tend to forget the basic activities that go into success in sales. Selling is very simple. It's about numbers and getting yourself in front of and talking to more people than anyone else. I'm going to show you how to do that.

Why Prospecting
is So Important

You know in a survey conducted among top sales people they were asked, "What percentage of your time, energy and effort were spent in the following four areas critical to sales success: prospecting, presentation skills, product knowledge, and personal and professional development?" And this is what those top producers said—50% of their time, energy and effort was spent prospecting, 20% in presentation skills, 15% on product knowledge, and 15% personal and professional development.

Now, what does this tell us? Well, to me, it says prospecting is the key. If you can't get in front of any prospects then none of your other skills matter because you won't get an opportunity to sell. You can deliver the most polished presentation in the world, know the features and benefits of your products and services backwards and forwards, and go to every seminar, read every sales book and listen to every audio program on the market.

But if you have no one to tell your story to, none of it matters. It's all about the numbers.

Prospecting is like a funnel. For example, you might make 30 calls; those 30 calls can yield you 15 contacts, which will get you 3 appointments to make 1 sale. And this could be your average because every salesperson has an average. And let me tell you this, it does not matter what your average is, what matters is that you know what it is, because only if you know what your averages are can you formulate a sales plan to get the amount of sales you need and earn the amount of money you need to make.

Let's face it, if you want to double your sales, double your activity. If you want to close 3 sales and know on the average that for every 30 dials of the phone, you'll speak to 15 decision makers, book 3 appointments, and close 1 sale, then all you have to do is make sure to make 90 calls. Or better yet, get 87 people to say no to you. I'll tell you this, it doesn't matter how many people say no, it only matters how many people say yes. So, why care about the no's? You don't get penalized for the no's, but you do get rewarded for the yes's.

How to Handle Rejection

Now that you understand the importance of prospecting, let's move on to handling rejection. And I'll get this right out upfront. Rejection stinks. I don't like it; no one likes it, and neither should you. Any sales trainer who ever tells you don't take it personally, just let it roll off your back, is one of two things, either an idiot or someone who has never sold anything. Everything in life is personal. And the reason we take rejection personally is we care.

But here's the big problem with rejection. I don't like it and neither do you, but in order to be successful we need lots of it. So, how do we handle it? Well, to me there's only one way to handle rejection, that's to know how much rejection you need.

You know, no's a rejection, but if you understand how many no's you need in order to make one sale, then no's are easier to take. There's a call counting system on pages 26 and 27 of the Action Guide at the end of this book, which you can use to understand how much rejection you need on average to make one sale. Now, the chart on page 26 will explain what each column represents. The chart on page 27 is a sample of the actual chart you should be using on a daily and weekly basis to track your activity.

This system will show you what your averages are, as well as what your success ratios are. To track your numbers, use the chart on page 27 on a daily basis, and then total those numbers up on a weekly basis. Keeping track of these numbers will do several things for you. One, it will allow you to save time. Two, it will allow you to make more money; that's a good thing. Three, it's going to enable you to avoid slumps. And four, it will help you to anticipate problems before they become critical.

Now, people always ask how long should I keep the numbers for and I say you should keep the numbers forever. But you won't see a true average until after three months of tracking these numbers. And after that three months, you will know, for instance, how many dials you need to get to one contact, how many contacts you need to get one appointment, how many appointments you need to get one sale, and how many sales you need to make x amount of dollars in commission. Now, at the beginning of the year, you can formulate a plan by asking what do I have to do on a daily basis, throughout the year to the end of the year with the amount of business that I want to come home with.

Let me give you an example of what I'm talking about. Far too many people start the year on the wrong side of the equation, especially sales people. They say, "This year if I make a lot of calls, I'll make a lot of sales." Then they come to work on January 2nd to start the year and the first three people they call say, "Drop dead." Guess what? The year is over. That's their allot.

The successful salesperson starts from the correct side of the equation. She might say to herself, "How much money do I need to earn this year to support the life-style my family and I choose to live?" Once she has that amount sorted out, it's easy to devise a plan expressing continuous action that will help her to achieve that goal.

Let's say for argument sake she decides she needs to earn $100,000 this year to support her and her family's lifestyle. She thinks to herself, "That's a lot of money. I've never earned that much before." But because she is a professional, she has kept good records and she has tracked her activity. She figured out that on the average, and every salesperson has an average, she earns $1000 commission for every sale. Now, she thinks to herself, "I don't have to earn $100,000; I just have to close 100 sales, or better yet, 2 sales a week."

"But hold it a second," she says, "it's not always within my power to close a sale.

Sometimes the prospect says no; sometimes they say something even worse, like I have to think about it. But not always, sometimes they do buy." And since she is a professional, who keeps records, she knows that she closes one of every three face-to-face appointments.

So, she doesn't have to earn any money, she doesn't even have to close any sales. All she has to do is make six face-to-face presentations a week. This job is starting to get a lot easier. But wait, it's not always within the salesperson's power to make sure the prospect or client shows up. Some of them don't show; some of them cancel, but not all of them. And because this young lady is a true professional, and has kept great records, she knows that she holds on to 75% of her appointments.

So, she doesn't have to make any money, doesn't have to sell anything. Heck, she doesn't even have to see these people. All she would need to do is set up eight appointments a week. Those eight appointments would yield six face-to-face presentations, leading to two sales at a $1,000 commission each, or $2,000 a week and $100,000 for the year.

So now the young lady who wants to earn this $100,000 realizes that all she has to do is set up eight appointments a week. But again, getting a decision maker to agree to see you is not 100% within the salesperson's control. Some people will say no; some will stall you. Some might even hang up on you, but not all of them. Since our salesperson in this scenario is a true professional, and keeps great records, she knows that one out of every five decision makers she speaks to gives her an appointment.

Now, let me get this straight. Don't have to make any money, don't have to sell anything, don't have to see anyone, don't even have to set up any appointments, I just have to speak to 40 decision makers a week. But you know? Not everyone gets on the phone; sometimes they end up speaking with a secretary or other gatekeepers.

Sometimes they get voice mail. Sometimes if I call the home office I might even end up speaking to a 9-year-old kid.

But we know that doesn't always happen. In fact, our $100,000 salesperson has figured out from her records that one out of every three times she physically dials the phone she gets to a decision maker.

So, now, hold on a second. Don't have to make any money; don't have to sell anything; don't have to see anyone or set up appointments. I don't even have to talk to these people. All I have to do is dial the phone 120 times a week, or 24 times a day, because if I do that, I'll speak to 8 decision makers a day, or 40 a week. I'll set up eight appointments a week, and actually hold six of them. Those six face-to-face presentations will yield me two sales on the average and put $2,000 a week in my pocket. That translates to $100,000 a year.

Now, how motivated do you think that young lady is to make the calls? You're right. She's a lunatic because she knows that every day she comes to work and gets 24 calls, she's getting that much closer to what she wants. She understands what every call is worth.

Now, even true professionals who track their numbers can run into slumps. Let's face it, slumps occur at certain times of the year with everyone. The beauty of tracking your activity and knowing your numbers is that you can figure out why slumps occur and fix only what's broken, because everything's broken down by categories.

For example, if the ratio of dials to contacts changes, you can change the time of day you call. If the ratio of contacts to appointments booked begins to fall, the problem may be a change you've made in what you're saying, or maybe you've stopped using your script, or maybe you're just winging it like so many sales people like to do, but that is so wrong.

Ratios are important; they can shorten your slumps.

How to Prepare for and Make the Prospecting Call

Now, we're ready to sit down and make our calls. But first, let's act like professionals and prepare. First, when preparing to make a call, you want to make a list of whom you're going to call before you begin your calling and put that list in front of you. Then, understand the purpose of your call is to sell the appointment. In fact, before every call you make, say to yourself, "What is the purpose of this call?" This will help you stay focused, concentrate on selling the appointment, and keep you away from selling on the phone which you don't want to do. Let's face it, in most cases you can't close the sale on the phone. The only thing you can do is lose it, so why get pulled into that trap?

Okay, now let's make the call, and in order to make a successful prospecting call you need to use a script. I know what you're thinking. "A script. I hate scripts. They sound canned. They're not me. I can't sound spontaneous." To that, I have one question.

Have you ever seen a Broadway show? Do you think they use a script? Did the script sound canned? I hope not, or if it did you paid to see a real lousy play.

But you know as well as I do they used a script and it didn't sound canned. And you know why that is? Because they practiced. Professionals practice; professional actors, professional athletes, professional musicians, they practice every day. As a professional salesperson, how often do you practice?

Let me tell you what a script can do for you. Number one, it allows you to control the conversation. And number two, it allows you to speak on the phone without having to think of what you're going to say. And if you don't have to think of what you're going to say next, you know what that allows you to do? It allows you to do something that far too many sales people and in fact, far too many people, fail to do, which is listen. And when a salesperson listens more effectively, they have a much better chance of hearing all the buying signals that the prospect's sending them.

So, now, let's put together a basic script that you can use to sell more appointments and increase sales. At the end of the book, there's a script in eight easy steps. Step number 1 of the script is to get the prospect's attention, and we do that by stating their name. So let's talk to Ms. Johnson today. So, we say, "Hello, Ms. Johnson." That's step number 1.

Step number 2 is to introduce yourself and your company. I would say, "Hello, Ms. Johnson. This is Warren Greshes from the Greshes Network." Now, the reason I ask you to use their name is because that is the easiest way to get someone's attention, and you need to get their attention because you're on the phone. They can't see you; it's easy for their minds to drift. Let's face it, most people don't have a long attention span and most people don't listen. So, we know that people react to their names more than anything else. If I yelled out your name in a crowded room, you would look up.

So, the first step is to get their attention by using their name. Second step introduce yourself and your company, third step, repeat their name because even by now, even after you've mentioned your name and your company's name, they're starting to drift away.

Get them back in; reel them back in. Repeat the prospect's name, "Hello, Ms. Johnson, this is Warren Greshes from the Greshes Network. Ms. Johnson."

And then step 4, give the reason for your call and one benefit to the prospect for seeing you. In other words, they want to know the same thing everyone in the world wants to know, and that is what is in it for me. So, you're going to tell them. If you can save them time, save them money, increase their business, tell them that. What I would say is, "Ms. Johnson, I'm calling today to tell you about our keynote speeches and seminars that could help your sales force and your company to increase their business."

If you believe that what you do can increase their business, save them money, make them money, save them time, then you have to tell them that because that's what they want.

Believe me, they want something that's going to benefit them and their company. I really believe I can do that.

So, I said, "Ms. Johnson, I'm calling today to tell you about our keynote speeches and seminars that can help your sales force and your company increase their business," and then I repeat her name again to make sure I've still got her attention, "Ms. Johnson."

And then step 6, I ask a yes question, and that's very simple. A yes question is are you interested in increasing your business? Are you interested in saving time, saving money?

Are you interested in your sales force increasing their business? Let's face it, if you get a no to that, you know what you do? You say, "Thank you very much, have a nice day."

Hang up quickly. Why? Because you don't want to argue with that person. Sure there are odds you can turn them around, but the odds are too great.

Aren't you better off just hanging up and going on to the next call? Remember, there's an average, keep going and you'll reach your average. Argue with people that don't want to buy from you or argue with people who are idiots, and you become the idiot. So if someone says no to me, "I don't want to increase my business." I just say, "Thank you very much. Have a good day." And I hang up.

But most people will say yes. And when they do say yes, you go to step 7 and show great enthusiasm and say, "That's great. Let's get together." And isn't that great? I mean, they're qualified, they want to increase their business, they want to save time, they want to save money.

Now we go to step 8 and this is the big one. You ask for a specific appointment. "That's great. Let's get together. How's next Tuesday at 3:00?" You want to ask for a specific day and specific time, because when you do that, a couple of things happen. Number one, you're taking control of the conversation. And number two, by giving the time and the date this shows that you are busy, and that you give the impression and you create the picture that you have other clients.

Remember, we're on the phone; we have to paint pictures for people. We have to create images for people. So, when you ask for a specific date and specific time, you're telling them you're busy. And when they know you're busy, they think you have other clients.

They know you have other things to do, and people want to buy from people that have other clients that are doing business. No one wants to buy from someone who says, "Let's get together. When is good for you?" Because a salesperson that says when is good for you has all the time in the world, which could mean no one is buying from them, which could mean they have no clients, and which could mean that what they're selling isn't worth buying.

Remember, most people will not do something unless they know that everybody else is doing it. And that's good, you want to let them know that you have other clients, that you are a busy person because people want to deal with a busy person.

Okay, now if the prospect responds with no to the specific time and date suggestion, just give another option. The beauty of asking for the day and the time is if they say no, you're not discussing if you're going to show up, you're just discussing when. That's called controlling the conversation. So, if they say no, when you say Tuesday at 3:00, just say, "Well, that's great. I can understand that because I'm busy, too. How's Wednesday at 4:00?"

Now, the prospect could say something else. They just could say, "I don't want to see you," or they could say, "Well, I already have that. I can't afford it. Could you send me some information?" You know what? You know what these are called? Objections.

And let's talk about turning around objections, which you will see at the end of the book in your Action Guide.

How to Anticipate, Handle, and Turnaround Objections

The best way to handle an objection is to repeat, reassure, and resume. In other words, first, repeat the objection; number two, reassure the prospect that it's okay to feel that way. Never argue with a prospect's objection; they don't know what they're supposed to know. That's not their responsibility; it's yours. You're the expert. And number three, resume, just keep on going. Remember you don't want to discuss the objection, you just want to discuss the day and time you're coming over.

Sales people tend to hear the same objections every day, yet because they're not prepared and don't use a script, each time they hear the same old objections, they act as if they've never heard it before. Let me ask you this. If you had the most common objections written down, and underneath each objection you had a turnaround, don't you think you would sell more appointments thereby delivering more presentations and closing more sales?

Well, guess what? That's what we're going to do talk about right now. Let's look at the first most common objection and that is when someone says, "Oh, I already have this."

You know what the best thing to say to that is? I would say, "That's great." And do you know why that's great? Because they do have it, they believe in it. They own your product or service. First of all, they know it costs money, they qualified. They use it. So I'd say, "That's great because you understand the benefits of what we would do." And then I would say, "But many of my clients said the same thing until I was able to show them, in person, how I could help them increase their business, how I could save them time, save them money."

And then, always come back to the close, which is, "Ms. Johnson, can we get together next Tuesday at 3:00?" Discuss the appointment, not the objection.

Now, let's analyze that turnaround. I said, "That's great because you understand the benefits of what we do." We already discussed that. It is great. When somebody already uses what you do or has somebody else, that's terrific. They believe in it, and they know it costs money.

And the second thing I said was, "But many of my other clients said the same thing."

And that's always a good turnaround to use because first of all it tells them you have other clients. It tells them their objection is valid because those other clients felt the same way, too, when they were just prospects. But then they saw the light, they saw how valuable doing business with you is. They saw that they could make money, save money, save time, increase their business. And now they've all come on board.

So, in other words, when you say they've all come on board, you're telling the prospect they've bought, it's okay for you to buy, too.

Now, let's move on to the second objection. The second objection to me is not valid at all, but a lot of people use it. They say, "I can't afford it." Now, that's not a valid objection because the prospect doesn't even know the price yet. But then again, too many sales people argue with that prospect. They'll say, "Well, you can't not afford it."

Well, that's stupid because you're assuming that they can afford it. And that's as bad as their assumption because you don't know whether they can or they can't either.

Instead, just say, "Ms. Johnson, I understand what you're saying. Many of my other clients said the same thing until I was able to show them in person, not only how I could make them money, but save them money." Then, "Ms. Johnson, can we get together next Tuesday at 3:00?"

Now, I know what you're saying, you're using the same turnaround for another objection.

Don't be afraid to use the same turnaround for more than one objection because I'll tell you right now, on any one phone call at most you're going to hear one objection. Do you really believe that you're going to hear four or five objections per phone call?

I know sometimes it feels like that but the beauty of the script is that when you use a script you can out prepare the prospect. Believe me, the prospects are not sitting there with a salesperson antidote script. And they're not going down the line of objections, and they're not sitting there thinking up new and better objections every day. They're coming up with the same ones all the time.

Now, let's go to the third one, the dreaded can you send me some information in the mail or can you email me something or can you send me to a website. Now, no one buys from information. But you have to be able to convey to the prospect a message that tells them why it's a greater benefit to see you rather than get the information in the mail. I mean, come on, they don't even look at the information.

So, you might want to say something like, "I would love to send you the information, Ms. Johnson. However, when I get there," notice when I get there, not if I get there, "you'll find that I'm much more qualified than the information is to answer any questions you may have and to be able to show you how I can help you increase your business. Ms. Johnson, can we get together next Tuesday at 3:00?"

See, you know as well as I do that you are more qualified than the information to answer questions and have more expertise than the information does. So, you've got to relay that message. But always remember, that you must always end your turnarounds with a specific time and date that you want to set up for the appointment.

Now, you could do this with any objections that you hear, any other objections. List the four or five or six most common objections you hear. Let's face it, I can't cover every objection in the book, but if you have the most common ones covered, if you have them written down, along with the turnarounds, this will keep your mind clear to handle any of the off-the-wall objections that you might hear. Remember out preparing the prospect is going to help you win far more often.

Now, what you want do with the script is type it up and type up the most common objections with their turnarounds, and type it up all on the same page so that it's easy to read and handle. The script itself is very short; it shouldn't take you more than 30 seconds to talk through it.

Why You Need to Practice Every Day

Let's talk about practice techniques. As I said before, professionals practice. You should be practicing every single day. Professional musicians practice three to six hours every day, just to give one lousy one to two hour performance. How many hours do you practice?

Another thing you should do is get yourself a timer. When you make your phone calls, time them because I don't want you to get in the habit of getting into what I call great conversations. You know those great conversations, the ones where sales people say, "Wow, what a great conversation. I think she really likes us." Did she buy anything?

Did she give you an appointment? "Well, she doesn't really need anything." Great conversations help to steer you away from the focus of the call. So, use a timer.

Get yourself a mirror. Place it on your desk in front of you. It's going to help you smile more because it's not the words you use but the tone of your voice. When you're a salesperson, you do not have the opportunity to be in a bad mood. The biggest obstacle to your success is you. All successful sales people share one common trait – their great attitude. And remember, on the phone, your prospects and clients can hear your attitude.

Now remember, reading *Don't Count the Yes's, Count the No's* can be quite motivating but simply reading, can't do a thing for you. Before the suggestions can have any real positive effect on your sales effort, they must be applied. To help you apply what you've learned, use the charts and exercises below to guide you through that important process.

Don't Count the Yes's, Count the No's is a great book. But it does nothing for you unless you actually apply what you've read and make that application a habit. So begin challenging your thoughts and building the roadmap that will make a significant difference in your sales career. I hope you become more successful than you already are.

Visit www.greshes.com.

Action Guide to
Effective Prospecting

Averages & Success Ratio Monitor
Week of: _____

DIALS	CONTACTS	APPOINTMENTS BOOKED	INTERVIEWS HELD	SALES	COMMISSIONS ($)
Tally here the number of dials you make.	Tally here the number of decision-makers you booked over the phone.	Keep track of how many appointments you booked over the phone.	In this column, keep track of the number of appointments you actually completed.	Tally the number of sales closed in this column.	Keep a running count of the commissions from your sales in this column, or total value of sales if you're not on commission.
TOTAL:	TOTAL:	TOTAL:	TOTAL:	TOTAL:	TOTAL:

Averages & Success Ratio Monitor
Week of: _____

DAY	DIALS	CONTACTS	APPOINTMENTS BOOKED	INTERVIEWS HELD	SALES	COMMISSIONS ($)
MON						
TUE						
WED						
THU						
FRI						
TOTALS:						

The 30-Second Script

Many salespeople make several big mistakes that can be easily corrected.

1. They don't decide who to call until they're actually making their calls.
2. They aren't clear on the purpose of their call.
3. They don't use a script. They have not practiced it or rehearsed it. Therefore, they are unprepared and unable to be clear, concise, and to the point.

It follows then that in order to make a significant difference in your success ratio on the phone, (the number of contacts that result in actual appointments) you need to do three things:

1. Prepare a list in advance of contacts to call.
2. Be clear on the sole purpose of your call (to make an appointment).
3. Prepare, practice, and rehearse a script that also includes prepared responses to your most common objections.

The first two things above must be done at another time. However, the third, the preparation of the script, you must do right now. Remember the primary benefits of a script?

1. It allows you to control the conversation
2. It allows you to speak on the phone without having to think of what you are going to say.

Phone Prospecting Script

On this page you will find the structural skeleton for your script. As you prepare it, visualize yourself talking to the prospect on the telephone.

1. Introduce yourself and your company:
   "_____(*Prospect's Name*)_____"

2. Repeating the prospect's name, give the reason for your call and one benefit to the prospect for seeing you.
   "_____(*Prospect's Name*)_____
   I'm calling because_____"

3. Repeat the prospect's name and ask a "yes" question:
   "_____(*Prospect's Name*)_____?"
   If the prospect says "no," say:
   "Thank you very much, ____(*Prospect's Name*)____.
   Have a good day."
   Hang up.

4. With a "yes" response, show Enthusiasm and ask for a specific appointment (day and time):
   "_____"

5. Plan your quick wrap up of your call:
   "Thank you, _____(*Prospect's Name*),_____
   I look forward to talking with you on____(date)____
   at ____(time)____"

(This is the time to confirm the date and time of your appointment. Avoid calling the day of the appointment to confirm, giving your prospect an opportunity to say, "Glad you called . . . I just can't make it . . .").

Objection Turnarounds

Remember, the best way to handle an objection is *Repeat, Reassure,* and *Resume.*

1. Repeat the objection.
2. Reassure the prospect that it's OK to feel that way.
3. The resume.

Now write the three most common objections you hear below. Then, write your planned turnaround below to each of the objections.

Objection #1: _____

    Turnaround:

        1. Repeat & Respond

        "_____*(Prospect's Name)*_____"

        2. Resume

        "_____*(Prospect's Name)*_____,
        can we get together next_____at_____?"

Objection #2: _____

    Turnaround:

        1. Repeat & Respond

        "_____*(Prospect's Name)*_____"

        2. Resume

        "_____*(Prospect's Name)*_____,
        can we get together next_____at_____?"

Objection #3: _____

  Turnaround:

    1. Repeat & Respond

    "_____(*Prospect's Name*)_____"

    2. Resume

    "_____(*Prospect's Name*)_____,

    can we get together next_____at_____?"

Congratulations! You're now prepared for your phone prospecting!

You will find it very helpful to retype this script, using all capital letters and double spacing. Try to include everything on one sheet of paper. If it doesn't completely fit with the objections, then type the objection turnarounds on a second sheet of paper and lay them side by side in front of you.

Finally, be sure to do as professionals in other fields do! Practice, practice, practice! Doing so will help you "perform" smoothly and easily.

Idea to Implement:		
Time Frame: Begin_____ Complete_____		
Order #	Tasks To Complete Implementation	Date To Be Completed

Idea to Implement:		
Time Frame: Begin_____ Complete_____		
Order #	Tasks To Complete Implementation	Date To Be Completed

Congratulations! You have done a lot of thinking and planning and you're ready to make some significant changes!

Be sure to use this blueprint and the charts you've completed to monitor and evaluate your progress. Remember, without written plans and a periodic review of those plans, your good intentions will remain good intentions.

Time Management Skills That Work

Time Management Skills That Work

Being great at time management, is hard. In fact, I'm not sure I know anyone who is great at it, but luckily you don't have to be. My goal for this book is not to make you a time management expert because I'm not really convinced you need to be. What I want to do is give you some easy to implement tips and ideas that will allow you to become a little more efficient on a daily basis.

If I can help you save 15 to 30 minutes a day, maybe I can help relieve a little bit of the stress that comes with your job and make you more productive. Some of these time-saving tips will also help you in your personal as well as your professional life, which is great since one of the goals of this book is to help you achieve a great life-work balance.

I want to make this program as simple as possible for you to follow and profit from, so what I'm going to do is break it down into two parts. In the first part, I'm going to give you a salesperson's time test. It contains ten questions relating to how you currently handle your time. When I pose these questions to you, I want you to be completely honest with yourself when you answer. After each question, I want you to take a second and write down whether this is something you do always, usually, sometimes, rarely, or never. The way you answer these questions will help you gain a tremendous amount of insight into where you need the most help in your personal and professional time management.

In the second part of this book, I'm going to address the areas we'll be covering with these ten questions and give you 20 very practical tips you can implement immediately that will help you save money, increase sales, and make your life and job a little more efficient, and a little less stressed.

So, let's get started. Here are the 10 questions.

1. Do you do things in priority order? Now remember, be honest with yourself. Is your answer always, usually, sometimes, rarely, or never?

2. Do you accomplish what needs to get done during the day?

3. Do you tackle difficult or unpleasant tasks without procrastinating? This is probably one of the toughest questions to answer "always" to. I know it is for me.

4. Do you prepare a daily plan and set priorities?

5. Do you get your paperwork done on time? I know I can honestly say I don't know anyone who loves doing paperwork. Do you? But once again, do you get your paperwork done on time?

6. Do you use your waiting and travel time effectively? I want to stop here for a second to clarify one thing. In the spirit of work-life balance, something I'm a big believer in, travel time can also mean commuting to and from the office. I'll get in to how use that more effectively later on. So, again, the question number 6 is do you use your waiting and travel time effectively?

7. Do you schedule your clerical work during low value time, instead of prime time?

8. Do you have a specific purpose for each sales call? By sales call, I mean both telephone calls and in person sales appointments.

9. Do you know how many calls per year are economical to make on each customer?

10. Do you take enough time to prospect and develop new business?

The purpose of these questions is to see where you are now in terms of your time management skills because only if you know where you are can you formulate a plan to get to where you need to be.

Now, score yourself, but before you do, I just want to say it's not important what your score is. What's important is that you know your capacity for improvement.

Here's how to score your answers. For any question you answered "always" give yourself five points. For each "usually," you get four points. For "sometimes," you get three points; "rarely," two points. And one point each time you answer "never."

Total up your points and if you scored 45 or higher, you are a time management superstar. If your score is 35 to 44, that's very good, but you could use some improvement; 25 to 34 means you could be heading for trouble. And a score of 10 to 24, well, let's put it this way, you have nowhere to go but up.

You know what's beautiful about this? You don't have to turn every score into a five. It's not necessary. If all you did was turn your 1's into 2's, and your 2's into 3's, and so on, you would easily save yourself that 15 to 30 minutes every day, making yourself more efficient and productive.

• • •

Okay, now that you've finished the test, let's get started and talk about those 20 time-saving tips. They are:

1. Prioritize. Decide on your long-term goals and set short-term priorities within those goals. You should have a clearly defined set of goals and plans for your life and career. Our goals and plans are what give us focus, direction, and a sense of purpose, which keeps us on track and less susceptible to people who want to take us in directions that will only waste our time.

When it comes to our long-term goals, the best way to achieve them is to first break them down into easier to accomplish short-term goals. Work with your manager to find out how you can use your job as a vehicle to achieving your goals, whether they be business or personal goals.

2. Concentrate. Eliminate self-made interruptions and distractions. Minimize interruptions imposed on you by others, especially phone calls, emails, and drop-in visitors. Other people are some of the biggest time wasters you'll face on a daily basis. Don't let them infringe on your time. Here's a tip to counteract people who like to drop in, sit down, and never leave. If you need to see them, go to their office or work space. This way, when you're done, you can get up and leave. You can't do that in your office.

If those drop-ins are actual prospects, naturally you don't want to hustle them out of there, but you do want to keep the conversations focused on the business at hand.

Eliminate great conversations and keep it to the purpose of the visit. Not only will you save time, time that can be used to get back on the phone, but you'll also save the client time, which I'm sure they'll appreciate.

Eliminate phone interruptions and email interruptions by not answering every call or email as they come in. Just like constant starting and stopping is not good for your car or your gas mileage, it's murder on your momentum or workflow during the day. Designate certain times of the day to return calls or emails, like early morning or late afternoon.

3. Break down major tasks into small ones, so that (A) the work is more manageable; (B) you can reward yourself as you complete each small step; (C) you can keep better track of your progress; and (D) you can avoid trying to do too much or doing things at the last minute. There's an old saying which goes, "How do you eat an elephant?" Of course, the answer is one bite at a time. Take any and all tasks and time them; see how long it takes to complete. Divide it by the amount of days you have to complete it and then get it done. You're always better off doing a little bit a lot rather than a lot a little bit. Let me repeat that. You're better off doing a little bit a lot rather than a lot a little bit.

It's just like your kids and their homework. I'm sure it drives you crazy when your kids have two or three weeks to study for a test or complete a project and they wait until the last second. I wonder how many of us, myself included, handle some of our work projects the same way.

When I first started my business, one of the many tasks I had a hard time keeping up with was the books. This was in the days before computers and Quicken. I had to do everything with pen and pencil in a big ledger book. Naturally I fell behind until I decided to do a little bit a lot. Each day I set aside 15 minutes to do the books, and within 10 days I was caught up.

Another benefit of doing it this way is the great sense of accomplishment you feel each day when you finish that 15 minutes. There's nothing like setting a goal and accomplishing it on a daily basis.

But, the biggest benefit of breaking major tasks into small ones and not waiting for the last minute to get them done is it avoids crisis situations. You know as well as I do, if we save a major task until the last minute, other emergencies will pop up that will make it impossible to get the project done on time. Now, I don't know what kind of emergency you'll encounter but I know there will be one. Why? Because there always is.

Alright, let's move on to the next tip.

4. List all upcoming commitments or important re-minders on one central calendar to facilitate planning. I don't care if you use a Blackberry, a Trio, your laptop, desktop, pocket day-timer, or a yellow pad, just as long as you use something, with the operative word being use because it doesn't matter how comprehensive your system is or how many bells and whistles it has. If you don't use it or if you write in it but don't look at it, it's useless.

5. Learn to say no easily and graciously. The word "no" is one of the greatest timesaving devices known to mankind. Make use of it. Now, don't take this to mean that you're supposed to say no to every request you receive throughout the day. And if you do, don't go saying, "Don't blame me. Warren's the one that told me to tell you no." What I'm saying is this, if you get 20 requests a day and normally say yes to all of them, I'm sure you can find one you can turn down based on your priorities. If you do, I'll bet that will save you the 15 to 30 minutes you're looking for.

6. Never do more than one major thing at any one moment, although you might shift back and forth among projects. Repeat after me, "Even though I think I can, I can't do more than one thing at a time." Do one thing at a time and do it well. If you get interrupted, and you will, leave it, concentrate on the new task, and then go back to it. Multi-tasking is a great skill but far too often it creates a lot of mediocre work.

7. Develop a system for tracking your daily activities, such as "a things to do" list. I love "things to do" lists, and I'm a big believer in them. But I also find that most people get a lot less out of their "things to do" list than they could.

Let me illustrate. Most people have "a things to do" list that's about as long as their arm. The problem with these lists is you're more concerned with crossing things out than you are with getting the important things done.

People love crossing things off their list, which means they're more likely to do the tasks that are easy, rather than the ones that are pressing. They also love showing other people how many things they've crossed off their list. But the real goal is to get the most important things done.

First of all, your daily "things to do" list should always be written up the night before. It should be the last thing you do before you leave work to go home, for two reasons. First, it allows you to hit the ground running as soon as you get to work.

And second, if you choose to write up your list when you arrive at work in the morning, what's going to happen on those days when you walk in the door and something unexpected happens that has to be taken care of right away? I imagine you'll be sitting down to put together your "things to do list" around 11:00 a.m., not exactly a good time to plan your day.

Next, when you start writing down your "things to do", put down everything you want. I don't care if the list is as long as your leg, but then, do this . . . prioritize each item with A, B, or C. A being the most important, absolutely have to get done items. B items are those of some importance but could wait. And those items with a C are low priority. Once you get to work the next day, start working on your A's. Do them one at a time and when you finish one, cross it off and go on to the next. Don't start your B's until you're finished with your A's. I guarantee you will never complete your entire list in any one day, but you will be getting the most important things done when they're supposed to be done, and not because they're the easiest to do.

Now, you're probably saying, "Hold it a second. What about the C's? They're not getting done." Don't worry about the C's, they'll get done when they become A's. They'll get done when they're supposed to get done, and again, not because they're easy to do.

8. Periodically review and revise your personal short-term and long-term goals. I like to review them every three to six months. First off, it's important so I can see how much progress I'm making and whether or not I'm doing a good job of following the plan. But it's especially important to review your goals to determine if they're still important to you. Let's face it, our lives change. What's important to us today might not seem as important six months or a year from now. If that's the case, revise the goal, change it or get rid of it and set a new one. If you keep your life on track, it will help you at work and vice versa.

9. Paperwork time is infinite; selling time is not. You can only sell when clients and prospects are around, but paperwork is a one person task that can be done even at 3:00 a.m. on Saturday morning. Now I'm not telling you to do paperwork at 3:00 a.m. Saturday morning, in fact, I don't want you to. I want you to have a life; I think that's extremely important, but you get the point.

Oftentimes there's no way around it, very few people in this world became successful working 40 hours a week. You wouldn't be the only person to put in extra time or take work home with you, but just remember, while working hard is a good thing, working smart is just as good, if not better. Why do paperwork if you can be talking to a client on the phone or in person? If you have to do paperwork during normal business hours, block out a certain time to do it. Don't do it as you're making phone calls. Try to avoid momentum breaking starts and stops.

10. If you don't know, ask someone who does. Boy, does this fall into the category of things that sound dumb but are true. Then why doesn't everybody do it? I guess it's because there are people who just can't admit they don't know something. But in a world where all sorts of information is right at our fingertips, if we're willing to put in the time to look for it, are you really doing yourself, the clients, or anyone else a favor by not digging for the correct information? Part of being an expert advisor, resource, and single point of contact is not your ability to know all the answers. Nobody does. It's your ability to get those answers in the quickest and simplest way possible.

11. Use downtime, like travel and waiting time, productively. There is nothing more unproductive than travel time or waiting time, though it doesn't have to be. If you're involved in inside sales, you don't have to worry about traveling to appointments or waiting to see clients and prospects. I doubt you have much downtime at all,

but there is some. The first thing I can think of is your morning and evening commute.

Even if it lasts only 15 to 30 minutes, there are still tasks you can do to not only make it productive but by doing it in your car, you don't have to do it when you can be doing something else, for instance, listening to personal and professional development programs. One of the benefits of podcasts and audiobooks is that they represent information that can be listened to anytime and anywhere. What better place than in the car? That's 20 to 30 minutes you use to improve yourself, and it will save you 20 to 30 minutes at some other time, allowing you to do a task that can't be done while driving. And no, I don't mean drinking.

If you're in outside sales, let's talk about travel and waiting times. Whether you're traveling between appointments or commuting to and from the office, travel time is the best time for personal and professional development. Audio programs are a great way to turn a non-productive task into something that can make you more successful. Many sales people I know listen to podcasts on the way to appointments, allowing them to implement the ideas immediately while still fresh in their minds.

Another way to be productive during travel time is to keep with you a short list of prospecting or client phone calls that need to be made. Whether you have it stored in your PDA, laptop, or pocket calendar, there's always time in between appointments to get in a few calls, calls that don't have to be made once you're back in the office.

Nowadays with cell phones there's no excuse for not getting in a few calls when you're between appointments.

Technology has given us the ability to use waiting time to our benefit. In fact, I'm writing this particular paragraph on my laptop as I'm waiting to get a haircut. I've written articles in doctors' offices, sent out invoices while waiting to see a client, and written speeches in hospital waiting rooms. Believe me, it beats reading the crappy magazines.

Always carry around at least one piece of paperwork, or at least one report that needs to get done. The next time you're waiting to see a client or prospect, be productive.

As long as we're discussing waiting time, let me give you a tip. Don't let a client or prospect abuse you by keeping you waiting for an inordinate amount of time. My rule of thumb is 20 minutes from the time of the appointment, and then, I'm out of there. After a 20 minute wait, I'll approach the receptionist or secretary and say, "I have other appointments, and I have no time to wait. Unless she can see me right away, I'm afraid we're going to have to reschedule." It's very rare that the appointment does not get rescheduled.

I've also laid down some very important ground rules. One, I will not be taken advantage of; any good client relationship must be win-win. Clients need someone to take advantage of, don't let that someone be you. Let the competition handle that role. There's an old saying in sales I learned over 30 years ago, let me pass it on to you. "The way you break a client in, is the way they're always going to be." Meaning, if a client knows you'll wait in the reception area for an hour before being seen, be prepared to do that every time you show up. Or, if you're the type of salesperson who drops their price far too quickly and easily, be prepared to always cut your price.

The second thing you've done by laying down the ground rules upfront is you've let them know you're busy. And believe me, there isn't a client in the world who wouldn't rather deal with a busy person than someone who has nowhere else to go.

12. Have a purpose for every call. Before you pick up the phone to make a prospecting or client call, before you walk in the door for your next appointment, say to yourself, what is the purpose of this call. Doing this will allow you to focus more clearly on your purpose and stop you from wasting time. For example, if you're calling to make an appointment to see a prospect or client, your focus should be on what time you'll be getting together. If you concentrate on this, you won't be dragged into selling over the phone, a real time waster since you can't close it over the phone, only lose the sale.

Whether you sell over the phone or in person, knowing the purpose of the call will help to keep the conversation shorter, allowing you to speak to more people. If you're seeing a potential client hoping to get them to ask you to come back with a proposal, then your purpose is setting up the follow-up appointment. Stay focused; have a purpose, and always work towards that purpose in every sales situation. You'll not only save time; you'll also increase your sales.

13. Handle a piece of paper once. Admit it, you hate paperwork. I know I sure do. I can procrastinate over the same piece of paper with the best of them. Have you ever found yourself picking up a piece of paper from the left side of your desk, looking at it, reading it, commenting about it to yourself most likely, and then gently placing it down on the right hand side of your desk? Then, a couple of days later, what do you do? Pick it up from the right hand side of the desk, look it over once again, make the same comment, and place it back down on the left hand side of the desk, where it all started.

I'll bet you have done this without even realizing it. I know I have, but here's the solution that just might break you of the habit. The next time you pick up a piece of paper for the very first time, tear off a little piece of the upper right hand corner. The second time you touch that piece of paper, tear off a piece of the upper left hand corner. Then every time you keep picking up that same piece of paper, tear off another corner. When you start seeing numerous pieces of paper without corners, I think the point will sink in because there'll be no denying it. Handle a piece of paper once and either take care of it, file it, delegate it, or get rid of it. Make a decision the first time.

14. Buy a wastebasket and use it. Now I don't think I can be any blunter than that. Stop being one of those people who hang on to things like newspapers and magazines because you never know. If there's something in that newspaper or magazine that's that important, cut it out and start a file. Otherwise, toss it.

If you can't bring yourself to do that, here's another solution. Get yourself a box and every time you have some newspaper, magazine, or any other piece of paper that must be held on to because you never know, throw it in the box. After one month, if you haven't gone back and looked at anything in that box, toss the entire box. All this extra clutter just makes it harder for you to find the things you really need, forcing you to waste precious time.

15. Live off peak. Frequent stores, restaurants, service centers or banks during non-rush or off-hour times. Don't go to the bank on Friday afternoons just to stand in line with everyone else. Try not to get on highways at the height of rush hour. In other words, don't do what everyone else is doing at the same time they're doing it. If you're going out to lunch, do it early or late.

16. Use time-saving services whenever possible, including shopping over the phone and online. I love the internet; it saves me gas, it saves me time. And it saves me from the horror of dealing with 16-year-old store clerks who wiped their noses on their sleeves. I live less than 2 miles from Staples, but I haven't bought a single office supply in a store in 20 years. I love bookstores, but the time and money I save buying from Amazon more than makes up for it.

Here's another idea if you're not already doing it. Pay all your bills online. Not only does it save you time, no more checks to write, it also saves you money. Most banks offer the service for free and you no longer need stamps. If you're worried about security, don't be. I recently went to a seminar on identity theft and the speaker said that it's safer to pay your bills online than to mail them.

One thing I've always hated doing is going to restaurants on special days, like Mother's Day, Father's Day, or New Year's Eve. Not only is every place crowded, but the prices are artificially jacked up and the food is never as good since they have to prepare for ten times more people than they're usually used to.

17. Figure out the best way to handle each situation, for example, by phone, email, or in person. Not every client needs to be seen in person once a month, or even called once a month. Determine how often a client needs to be contacted and how, using a formula, that includes how much business they're doing with you, how much potential business they're capable of doing, and the odds of you tapping in to that potential.

Let me give you a little tip about email. I love email, but I think too many sales people use it as a crutch thinking that they're really selling via email, when all they're doing is participating in the illusion of selling. The reason so many sales people love email is that it's a nice, comfortable "no." You never actually have to hear the word. Nothing beats personal contact, whether in person or on the phone. What I like email for is as an add-on to personal contact. Email is a great way to keep your name in front of a prospect or client in a non-threatening way when you can't be calling or seeing them. It's a marketing tool. It's a great way to get information to people, but nothing beats the phone or a visit when it comes to actually closing sales.

18. Promise less, deliver more. Sales people get into more trouble trying to impress a potential customer by promising something they can't possibly deliver. They then end up wasting more time trying to clean up the mess they made and trying to win the client back. Do you know what clients like more than anything? The truth. It's a lot easier to remember. By promising less and always delivering more, you constantly look like a hero to your clients.

19. Prepare your outbound calls before you make them, not as you're making them, and know what you're going to say ahead of time. Do you want an easy way to save time making outbound calls? Prepare tomorrow's list of calls before you go home at night. Remember tip number 10? Paperwork time is infinite; selling time is not. There are only certain times of the day when you can be calling for business, don't waste that precious time by stopping after every call to figure out who you're going to call next.

Another great way to save time is to use a phone script. I'm a big believer in phone scripts. What's great about a script is that it allows you not to have to think about what you're going to say next, while the prospect or client is speaking. Which means, you're freed up to listen.

My favorite thing about a script is it allows you, the salesperson, to control the conversation. This is critical since you are the expert and it's your obligation to educate the clients and help them figure out what their needs are and how you can fill them. A script also allows you to out-prepare the person on the other end of the phone. I know sometimes it feels like the prospects and clients are sitting there with salesperson antidote scripts. But believe me, they're not.

The biggest problem with a script is that many sales people who use them sound canned, and there's a very good reason for that. They don't practice. If you've ever been to a Broadway show you know as well as I do that they used the script, but it didn't sound canned. You know why? They practiced. In fact, they practiced and rehearsed every day for months. You know why? Because they're professionals. You're a professional, too, and professionals practice.

Now here's our last tip, number 20. Prepare your strategy before you walk out the door. It's no secret that when you out prepare your opponent you give yourself a much better chance to win. Just as in tip 19, when you're preparing for the call, you also need to prepare for client interactions, whether onsite meetings, calls, projects, etc.

Just like when you set goals, begin with the end in mind. What's your purpose or desired outcome? Two, what's theirs? What agenda discussion items will help to drive to the desired result? What information can be provided ahead of time to give any background/knowledge necessary to enhance discussion and maximize results? What information needs to be gathered to support recommendations and strategy and reinforce the case? And how, when, and in what format should it be presented? Anticipating and delivering results and preparing a supporting strategy reduce rework and multiple follow-ups and fixes.

I hope I have given you some things to think about and some ideas that you'll put into practice. Don't try to do everything at once; just take one good idea at a time and run with it. Remember what I said at the beginning of this book? It's not necessary to be a time-management expert.

Find two or three good ideas out of the many I've covered here, and let each one of them save you 10 to 15 minutes a day. If you do that, your days will seem just a little less stressful. Your productivity will increase. Life will become just a little bit better, and there's nothing wrong with that.